The Small Business Jigsaw

The Small Business Jigsaw

How To Plan, Grow, And Love Your Business

Lucy Dempster & Julie Hayward

Published 2014
in Great Britain,

ISBN: 978-1500187477

British Cataloguing Publication data:
A catalogue record of this book is available from
the British Library

This book is also available as an ebook.

Please visit
www.thesmallbusinessjigsaw.co.uk
for more details.

With thanks to Scott, Jemma, Jack, Kirk and all the family and friends who continue to support us along the way.

Contents

Why We Wrote
'The Small Business Jigsaw'

In 2013 we decided that this was going to be the year that we focussed on our businesses. We took it in turns to set tasks that challenged us in every area of our business, from design to sales, profitability to life-work balance.

We didn't always choose tasks that we both wanted or enjoyed doing – sometimes one of us picked a task they knew the other would normally avoid – but it was glaringly obvious that it would be beneficial and had to be embraced. One thing we did notice was as we did those tasks we often started to enjoy them.

Somehow we remained friends :)

The plan wasn't to write a book but as we saw results we realised we'd produced something that could be valuable to other small businesses, so the writing began.

Introduction

The Small Business Jigsaw will take you through 21 main tasks and a number of bonus tasks that will prove invaluable whilst you plan, grow and love your business.

If you commit to working through the book you'll be amazed at the results. Work through every task even if you think it's one you've already mastered, it doesn't apply to your business or you don't have the confidence to do it. You'll get something from every chapter.

You will enjoy some tasks far more than others, and this is because they take you out of your comfort zone. It is for this reason that they are likely to have the greatest impact on your business.

There is no set timetable for working through this book. Some tasks will take longer than others and you'll find you need to continually revisit each one as your business evolves and its needs change.

There is a notepad page at the end of each task for you to make your initial notes.

If you feel you need extra support on the technical tasks, we've provided links on our website which will give you further guidance.

Get ready to do some hard work. The more effort you put in the more you will get out of it.

Task 1: First Things First

What is your business? What do you want from it? What are you prepared to give to achieve this?

Your first task is to strip your business to its bare bones so you know exactly what you're offering, what you want to get back and how much time, money and work you are willing to put in to achieve it. **You get to choose everything**.

This is your business. No one else can decide what you sell, how many hours you work or what makes it a success.

Are you going to concentrate on selling one service to a niche group of customers or a wide range of products to a mass market?

What made you start your business? A passion to help people? Enough extra income for days out or to pay for a millionaire's lifestyle? Or something else?

Do you want a chain of shops or a maximum of four hours' work on a Wednesday afternoon?

Are you happy working every waking hour for that yacht or is spending time with your family more important?

What exactly *do you want* to be doing or selling? It's your choice.

To do:

Using the notepad page at the end of this task, devise a Wish List for your business. Answer the questions above and include things like the hours and finance you're happy to commit, the income you want to achieve and the lifestyle benefits you want, such as money, time and freedom. Don't be afraid to think big.

Our experiences:

> *Lucy: "I have been running my business for 18 years. Initially I wanted it to fit around a full time job and then around my young family. In the last few years I had more time and wanted to take it from something that 'fitted in' to a full time business. It was whilst approaching things from this new perspective I realised I could make big changes by implementing simple tasks. It also showed how a business can start as one thing and evolve to fit in with my changing lifestyle."*

Julie: "My business needs to pay all of my bills and give me enough extra for luxuries. To earn a good wage I know that long hours are vital but I'm not prepared to let work become more important than my partner, family and friends. They will always take priority. I soon realised that managing my working week so that everything gets done and life can still be flexible is key. This new perspective led to some vital changes in the way I work."

Notepad

Task 2: Professional Branding

What image are you projecting? Is it professional? Is your branding good enough to be mistaken for a national corporation?

This task is about presenting the right image. Regardless of how big or small you are, whether you work in your spare room or rented offices or how many people work for you, you need to make similar branding decisions to those of a multinational company.

Branding is about creating the right name, logo and design - they should all get right to the core of your business.

Take a look at your current company colours, logo and name. If a potential customer saw your brand would they know what you do, how you do it and your level of expertise? You know what you're trying to portray but is the message getting across? If you're an accountant your branding needs to tell the world you're brilliant – it doesn't need to give any indication that you're working from your kitchen table. Clients just need to know you are as good as the best City accountancy firm – if it suits you to work from home that's up to you.

Your brand design will be used across all forms of media – stationery, website, social networking and advertising – so you need to get it right. This doesn't necessarily mean spending thousands as depending where your skills lie you may be capable of designing this yourself. If not, the right professional help doesn't have to cost a fortune. Your name and logo really are important.

To do:

Find out if what you already have is right for you – ask honest friends, clients and other professionals what impression they get from your current branding. If it's right, use it everywhere.

If it's not right change it so that it puts the right message across. If you can't do it yourself employ a professional.

Our experiences:

Lucy: "When I refurbished my clinic I realised my business, even after 16 years, didn't have a name! I wanted to show that I was professional about my work.

I researched logo designers and found a fantastic company (www.verveprint.co.uk) who charged a reasonable price for an amazing product. My logo now says everything I want it to – my name, what I *do – it's in my colours and it has the look I want to portray. I've used it for business cards, loyalty cards, after care leaflets, website design, social networking sites and my blog and I now feel I am projecting a more professional image."*

Julie: "When I looked at my logo I loved it. However, I knew I could improve on it. A friend of mine suggested changing the photograph of my Balloon Baboon into a cartoon character. For very little outlay I found someone to do just that and I love the result. I now have a much cleaner image that sits well on my website, leaflets, Facebook, Twitter, Pinterest, newsletter, blog and stationery."

BONUS TASK: FIND A BUDDY

It is useful to have someone to talk to when you run your own business. It gives you the chance to get another opinion on everything, big or small.

- Find someone who you trust and who has their own business too so you can support each other in person or online
- Use each other as a sounding board
- If you tell your buddy what you're setting out to do you're more likely to commit to achieving it.
- Celebrate milestones and successes with each other
- Treat everything you talk about in confidence

Notepad

Task 3: Your Competition

Who offers the same products or services you do? What, exactly, do they offer and at what price? What makes you the same and uniquely different?

During this task research the companies that are similar to you and identify which you are in competition with. Depending on the nature of your business they may be local, national or global companies. Once you know who they are find out what they do, how they do it and the price they charge.

What makes you better than your competition? It could be that you both sell the same product at the same price but yours comes wrapped in tissue and in an elegant bag. You make slightly less profit but may be more likely to create a repeat customer or some invaluable word of mouth advertising. Similarly, you and your competitor are both highly qualified electricians charging the same rate. However, you always answer your phone and turn up when you say you're going to, giving you a better reputation. There will be similar businesses with very different approaches to yours. You can learn from the good and the bad.

It isn't just about being different. There may be things you like about your competition, and these are things you should develop and adopt. Don't just try to be better than the average; aspire to be as good as the best.

To do:

Identify similar businesses to yours. Call, visit, order from or use the companies you've highlighted. What would make you want to use the best companies and avoid the worst?

Our experiences:

Lucy: "I have regular treatments in other salons and make note of the good and bad to help my business. I have had massages in cold rooms, which meant I couldn't relax, so I always ensure the room temperature is right for the client in my clinic. I have also seen smart, spa-like salons which became my inspiration when I redesigned my clinic."

Julie: "I ordered a delivery from a competitor to go to a friend. She was disappointed as one of the balloons was deflated. Deflated balloons are unacceptable so we now rest everything overnight to ensure there are no defects. It means that we can't offer same day dispatch but we explain this to customers by telling them that we want our sculptures to arrive in perfect condition. They seem to appreciate our commitment to high standards over speed.

To make us stand out all of our balloon deliveries come with a little Balloon Baboon sculpture that holds a personal message from the sender. It makes it far more personal and ensures we are remembered. Almost every 'thank you' we get mentions him and how cute he is."

Notepad

Task 4: Setting Targets

What do you want to achieve in the coming year?

In *First Things First* (Chapter One) you had the vision, and you worked out what you wanted your business to be and what you were willing to commit to achieve that vision. Now it's time to put in the hard work so you can make that dream your reality. It's time to set targets.

This task focuses on where you want to be one year from now. You may need to look at where you want to be in five years' time and then work backwards so that you know what you need to do this year.

Your targets may be based around money – earning £20,000 a year or being debt free; it might be changing premises – moving out of your spare room and into an office; or they could be about growth – you may want to employ staff this year so that you can work less and spend more time with your children.

Your one year targets should take you closer to your final goals. You may have more than one target if you have several goals. Think hard. Your targets need to be specific; only then can you figure out exactly what you need to do to achieve them.

Don't worry if you want to change your targets along the way – keep reassessing them. As your business develops you may want to take things in a different direction.

To do:

Write your one year targets on the notepad page of this task. Put a copy of them where you can see them so you are constantly reminded of what you are aiming for – decorate them, put them in a fancy box or on a piece of paper in your wallet, whatever works for you.

Our experiences:

Lucy: "When I studied reflexology in the '90s I was taught that people shouldn't have treatments if they had conditions such as cancer. I made it one of my targets to push into this area. Many years later I have a Diploma in Complementary Therapies in Cancer Care from The Christie Hospital and I volunteer at my local hospice. This is something I would never have done had I not set those initial targets."

Julie: "I really enjoy making balloon sculptures but my background is in sales and marketing. There are far faster balloon twisters so it makes sense to employ them rather than making the designs myself.

*That way I can concentrate on what I do best -
marketing. So one of my targets this year is to
employ a balloon twister to take on most of the
actual manufacture. I already employ help at busy
times like Valentine's and Mother's Day but the aim
is to employ someone all year round."*

Notepad

Task 5: Breaking Down Your Targets

How are you going to achieve your targets?

You set your targets in the last chapter. Some may seem massive and a little overwhelming, but honestly, they're not. Break down each task into manageable chunks and you will be moving towards those targets in no time at all.

Pick one of your targets – for example, to be earning £20,000 a year. If you want to achieve this in two years, work out where you should be at the end of the first year: perhaps earning £10,000. What would you need to earn each month to achieve that? How many sales is that a month? A week? What do you need to do to find those customers – networking both online and offline? Door to door leafleting? Editorial in your local paper?

Alternatively, imagine you set up a children's clothes shop on eBay; the target is to fund more days out with the family. To sell more you need to find out what sells, how to find those clothes at the best price and quality and advertise what you have – in that order. Your first step is to research the market, brands, age range, styles that sell. Then move on to the next step: buying them at the right price.

To do:

Take one target at a time from *Setting Targets* (Chapter Four) and break it into manageable chunks or mini tasks. Focus on each mini task, defining the steps you need to reach it. Work through each step.

Our experiences:

Lucy: "I wanted to extend and upgrade my clinic. I found out what it would cost to build, what products and furnishings I would need and how much extra work I would need to do to cover costs. I researched the products I would like to use and if they were affordable for a small business. I also looked at colour schemes, fixtures and fittings. Once the capital was raised everything else quickly fell into place because I had broken the initial 'big-build' down into small chunks."

Julie: "Wanting to achieve X number of sales a month means increasing exposure of our products online. The national sites that sell some of our products will always have a far bigger audience than we will. Every product they feature gets great exposure and through that a high volume of sales, so it makes sense to create new products that are right for their audience. This is just one of the small steps we can take towards hitting that monthly target."

Notepad

Task 6: Stock Take Time

How much money are you holding in stock? Can you reduce it and put the money back in your pocket?

For this task you are going to do a thorough stock take. You need to count EVERYTHING in every drawer, cupboard, nook and cranny. If you are a beautician this will mean every nail varnish, cotton wool pad and bottle of acetone. If you make greeting cards it will mean every pack of paper, embellishment and tub of glitter.

Looking at the items you have, do you notice anything? Do you have some stock that is getting dusty in the back of a cupboard? Do you have products that are already open but hardly used? Do you have some items that are overstocked or going out of date? Now is the time to figure out how to convert this dead stock into money – you'll be surprised at how much money is actually sitting around doing nothing.

How can you reduce your stock? Could you do any special offers? Maybe two for one or 20% off? Could you devise new products or services that use stock in a new way – maybe, a new range of boys' birthday cards to use up that blue card and some of those car or dinosaur embellishments? Can you promote your services more effectively so you always sell products before they go out of date? For example, facial products have a shelf life. That luxury £55 facial should be promoted regularly so that you don't open a jar of your most expensive moisturiser for just one customer. This will not only reduce expensive wastage but also increase revenue.

There might even be items that you no longer use or need. If you're a handyman do you need a spare drill and a spare-spare drill? There may be things you can sell, throw out or just give away to give you more room and a healthier bank balance.

And next time you're placing an order think hard about what and how much you are ordering.

To do:

Using paper or a spreadsheet, do a stock take. Include everything and identify what you don't need and what you have too much of. Next, come up with a strategy to turn that stock into space and money. Buy future stock with care and keep your stock list up to date.

Our experiences:

> *Lucy: "I had way too much stock. Did I really need a spare bottle of every CND shellac colour when some*

weren't as popular? I started to wear some of the colours I had too much of and used them in layering combinations so that clients could see just how good they looked. I also started a log of how often I used each colour. As I knew how many applications were in a bottle it meant I could replace them just before they were empty. In 12 months I reduced my stock value from £1200 to £300, leaving me more money in my cash flow."

Julie: "Very often we need to buy a bag of balloons in a particular size or colour for a new design. Whilst doing our stock take it became obvious just how many bags of balloons we had with just one or two taken out of them. It was tying up a lot of money. We took our list of underused balloons and decided to design some new sculptures that would use them up. Some of our most popular designs have come out of sessions like this. They not only used up bags of balloons that would otherwise have perished but they also created some great new products that sell well to this day."

BONUS TASK: SOURCING STOCK

The best deal for you may not be the cheapest
- Look locally, nationally and internationally; online and offline
- As your business changes constantly reassess your options
- Build a relationship with your supplier and take advantage of their expert knowledge
- Don't overstock

Notepad

Task 7: Yes or No

How many business decisions do you make a week? How do these decisions impact on you and your business? Are you making the right decisions?

What decisions do you make each week? I bet you included whether to take out that newspaper advertisement or book that course. But did you also include all the day to day decisions that you also make, such as whether you really needed to respond to that text at 9.30pm or whether you should increase an order to get free postage?

This task is all about the consequences of your *Yes* or *No*. For example, you need to order one item at £6 but delivery is £5; however, if you spend £60 delivery is free. Your instinct might be to spend the extra and save £5 postage because you'll use the stock eventually, but do you really need to? Is this how you ended up with surplus unsold stock that sits on the shelf, goes out of date or out of fashion and leaves you with less money in your bank account? You now need to question every purchase.

Remember that client who sent a text at 9.30pm whilst you were out having dinner with your husband. You thought: "Great, a potential new client," so you replied. Thirty minutes and five texts later your dinner has gone cold and so has the atmosphere. Would you really have lost that client if you'd waited until the morning? This is your business and you need to control it – not the other way round.

To do:

Question every decision you make, however big or small. Make sure your decisions are informed rather than impulsive. Start to question the benefits and consequences of every *Yes* or *No*.

Our experiences:

Lucy: "I realised I was saying yes *to the things I like to do and* no *to the things that took me out of my comfort zone. I had to start learning to say* yes *if it was for the good of my business. I was asked to write an article for a training company and I kept telling myself, "No, I can't do this." During this task I said* yes *and found I actually loved writing again. I even started writing this book! In addition, people who read the article then visited my website."*

Julie: "I really wanted to do a course that would teach me how to make miniature candy trees for our balloon characters to hold so I booked one. I thought I could increase income by offering this as an add-on to our balloon sculptures. During this task I decided to say no and cancel my place. It was coming up to Mother's Day, a busy time, and I would be better off using this money to advertise and buy stock."

Notepad

Task 8: Weakest Links

Which elements of your business are letting you down? What could you do better and how could you make changes?

During this task look at how you do things in every area of your business. That includes how you deal with customers – from the first time they contact you right through to aftercare, and your product range – how do you develop, produce and advertise it?

Some things will be working perfectly. Others might be a problem, costing you time and money. Even worse, they could be losing you customers. Your weakest links are things that stop you reaching your full potential. Some will be simple and solved quickly; others may be larger.

If you work from home, how professional do you appear? What impression does it make if your five-year-old picks up the phone to a customer? Does it have a negative impact? Alternatively, during the creation of your website you might not have included an online cart as you assumed it wouldn't be needed. You've since received several calls asking for just such a facility. Your gorgeous website that you spent so long creating is now a weak link as it's not fulfilling your customers' needs.

Weak links are lurking in every business. It's your job to scrutinise everything, find them and fix them. Your weakest links might be things that take you out of your practical or emotional comfort zone. Maybe your IT skills aren't proficient so you haven't put as much effort into Twitter and Facebook as you could, or you may not be confident speaking in groups so avoid networking meetings.

Weak links could be in areas where you're stuck in your ways and haven't researched new product lines or ways of doing things. If you've always done something the same way you need to be sure it is the 'best way' and not just comfortable.

Equally, a member of staff may be a weak link. Are they fully trained? How can you support them so they move in the same direction as you?

As you solve one weak link, you may discover others. As with many tasks in this book, this is ongoing and you need to come back to it again and again.

To do:

Identify the weakest links within your business. Now is the time to act and turn them into your strongest attributes.

Our experiences:

Lucy: "Despite setting up Facebook and Twitter I was struggling to think of things to write and I'd often go months between posts. My weakest link was definitely social media! I challenged myself to write two tweets a day and post on my Facebook business page several times a week. I was shocked when I started to enjoy it and gained new clients. Pushing myself out of my comfort zone has really moved my business forward."

Julie: "We had a really great website which had images of all our products and clear, concise information about each one. However, we just couldn't find a web cart that was capable of collecting all the different bits of information we need for each delivery. Every time we thought we'd found a solution it let us down and we were back to square one. It wasn't something we could compromise on but it meant our fantastic website was as good as useless. Eventually we used an IT expert to create a bespoke cart and orders are now flowing in again."

Notepad

Task 9: The Jobs You Avoid

What jobs do you keep putting off? Do they start to feel overwhelming the longer you leave them? Is your procrastination holding you back?

This task is for all those little things that really get to you. They may only be small but you keep thinking about them rather than doing them. A good example is that bill on the desk that you need to pay, which has been there for two weeks as you keep thinking "I'll do that later." When you finally phone to make payment the office is closed so you try again on Monday morning and are now too late to get your early payment discount. How long do you spend thinking "Aahhhhhhh I must do that!" about the smallest of things – and what are the consequences?

Not doing that little job could be stopping you from taking the next step and moving forward. If you don't make that phone call to your supplier, you won't get that new product on your website in time for Father's Day.

These jobs may be small but the potential time and energy you lose is often disproportionate to the task in hand. Once you actually decide to tackle a job you are likely to find it doesn't take long and probably isn't as bad as you thought. Stop wasting emotional time and energy and just do it!

There will always be jobs you don't like or don't think you're very good at. These are the ones you should look out for, as they can easily end up becoming the things you waste energy trying to avoid. Recognise these, nip them in the bud and take action before they start to seem insurmountable.

If you keep putting off doing your accounts as you dislike them try scheduling them into your diary once a week so they don't build up. If you are avoiding something because you don't think you're very good at it, invest in some training or practice.

If it's a large job you're avoiding, don't panic! Just break it into manageable chunks – like you did with your goals in *Breaking Down Your Targets* (Chapter Five). Concentrate on the first step for now and that will set you off in the right direction.

To do:

Make a list of the jobs that you are putting off, grouping similar tasks together so they can be dealt with at the same time. Complete at least one job or step each day, more if you can. Identify which jobs you tend to avoid and implement a strategy so you don't have the same problem in the future.

Our experiences:

> Lucy: *"I used to dread doing my accounts. I would put each receipt in a pile and watch it getting bigger and bigger. Every time I saw it I would panic. During this task I realised I was wasting time and energy panicking and putting off the accounts again and again. I decided to confront my receipts every week and soon found that writing up weekly accounts was much easier than trying to remember what I had spent or earned several months before. I continue to do this and my accounts are now submitted months earlier than the deadline."*

> Julie: *"In 2013 we introduced a loyalty scheme. Customers collect points every time they place an order. 10 points can be exchanged for a free delivery up to a certain value. Administering the system is quite fiddly and time consuming so it often gets left at the bottom of each week's to do list. We now*

*schedule this task into the diary so that it is
completed on a regular basis. Keeping it up to date
shows customers that they are appreciated – why
have a loyalty scheme otherwise?"*

Notepad

Task 10: Facebook

Have you got a Facebook page? If not, why not? If you have one, does it reflect your business voice? Have you incorporated your logo and colours? Is your page active?

Love it or hate it – you can't ignore Facebook. It is free and an effective form of advertising if you use it properly. This task isn't about how to create a Facebook page; it is about how to use it effectively, making sure it reflects the corporate identity you created in *Professional Branding* (Chapter Two).

A successful Facebook page is a busy page. It is one where you post regularly and have lots of active 'likers' who want to share, 'like' or comment on your posts. They will get involved if they like what you post or feel they have a good relationship with you.

What makes a successful post?

> ➢ Facebook loves photographs. The more visual you can make your page the better. It gives 'likers' something to talk about.

> ➢ Questions encourage interaction.

> ➢ Showing a glimpse of the people behind the
>   business works – it's nice when a Facebook page
>   is obviously written by a human being.

> ➢ Exclusive offers, product previews and sneak
>   peeks all work well.

> ➢ Timing is important – you need to post when
>   your 'likers' are online.

Posts need to be regular – you don't want people to
forget you. And when they 'like', comment or share
your post, interact. Facebook is a two-way conversation
so respond to people and be interested in what they have
to say on their pages too. However, don't post too often
as you don't want people to feel you're spamming them.

There is nothing worse than staring at a blank screen
whilst trying to think of something interesting or witty
to say. Make an active list of posts you can write; start
collecting photographs or images you can use to make
your Facebook page come alive. Don't forget you can
access your Facebook account from almost anywhere if
inspiration hits you and you have a smartphone or tablet.

To do:

Create a Facebook page if you don't have one. It needs the right name and should be branded with your business logo and colours.

Get posting regularly, interact with comments and make sure people know you have a Facebook page and where to find it!

Our experiences:

> Lucy: "I used to find Facebook difficult to use. I felt I was talking to myself as I had little interaction from other people. After some research, I found a local networking page, Cheshire Ladders UK, which was a place where I could go for help, support and interaction with other local businesses. It gave me a chance to see how people were using their business pages by liking, sharing and commenting on other people's posts and I found out more about what people were doing in my own community. The more I used Facebook the more popular my page became and now it is a great tool for keeping in touch with clients."

Julie: "Out of all the posts we put on Facebook we find that photographs get the most response. It is a quick and easy way to advertise a new design and we often sell these on pre-order before they even make it to the website."

BONUS TASK - FACEBOOK

Facebook can be used for far more than just posts and pictures. You can:
- Run competitions
- Use your audience for market research and post links to surveys
- Consider starting a Facebook group for people with similar interests

If you feel you need extra support setting up a Facebook business page visit www.thesmallbusinessjigsaw.co.uk

Notepad

Task 11: Twitter

You have a Facebook page – do you have a Twitter account and are you tweeting regularly? It's not a choice – you need both.

Twitter is quick, easy, free and is great for small businesses. By increasing awareness of your business via Twitter you can drive users to your website and increase sales.

To be a successful tweeter you need followers. There's no point putting your message out there if no one reads, re-tweets or replies. You need to engage with followers by replying and re-tweeting their messages as well as encouraging them to respond and pass on yours.

Don't panic! You don't have to build a relationship with every one of your followers. Use your time wisely and concentrate on those who are, or potentially could be, your most influential fans. If your company is national this might be someone with lots of followers. If you're local it could be someone who lives nearby and re-tweets to their friends.

Tweets need to get straight to the point as they are only 140 characters long.

What will encourage people to read, re-tweet or reply?

- Something that makes them smile – be fun, friendly and inoffensive

- When you re-tweet add a comment to encourage a relationship

- Be visual – tweet photographs and images

- Don't just talk about yourself – conversations are two way

- Tweet regularly or people will forget you, but tweet too often and they'll ignore you

Use your time wisely. If you've tried to interact with someone and they're not responsive then don't be offended; move on. There are millions of other people on Twitter and plenty will gladly tell the world about your business.

You can tweet about anything and everything. If you don't know what to say, reply to other tweets and get chatting. Keep it light, dive in and you can't go far wrong.

To do:

Set up your Twitter account with the perfect name for your business and brand your home page with your logo and business colours. Look for the best people to follow.

Don't overthink this next one...start tweeting! Promote the fact that you tweet.

Our experiences:

Lucy: "Twitter has been one of my most effective social media tools. I may not have as many followers as other users but because many are local to me each one is worth their weight in gold. If I have a cancellation I can tweet it and it often gets filled. It's also made me aware of what's happening in the local area, which has helped me to support other local businesses and feel more involved in my community."

Julie: "Our sculptures are obviously very visual. Twitter is a perfect way of showing off new designs and with a few re-tweets thousands of people can see something we've just created. A couple of years ago we made a caricature of Alan Carr and left it at the stage door for him when he was performing locally.

He tweeted a picture of it and within a few days over 100,000 people had clicked on the link to get a better look at what we'd made. It was incredibly influential free advertising."

BONUS TASK - TWITTER

As with Facebook, you can make far more use of Twitter than you think.
- Run competitions
- Use your audience for market research and post links to surveys

If you feel you need extra support setting up a Twitter account visit www.thesmallbusinessjigsaw.co.uk

Notepad

Task 12: Websites

Have you got a website? Does it reflect you and your business? Is it easy to use?

Your website should perform all the tasks you need it to, perfectly. It is your shop window to the biggest and pickiest audience there is. If they don't like your site, it's too slow or hard to navigate, then they won't use it.

Your website needs to represent your brand – so use those colours, logo etc.

Decide what your website needs to do. Is it going to give a taster or answer every question your customers can think of about each product or service you sell? Do you want them picking up the phone to find out more or committing to an appointment online?

Consider the words you use. The right copy will turn browsers into customers. The way you express yourself is part of your company branding. If you're a local cab firm you'd need to come across as friendly whereas a solicitor needs to be more formal. Your words will give your customer that all-important first impression, and an insight into the personality of your business.

Once you know what you want your website to do, and depending on your own expertise, you may decide to build it yourself. Do your research if you prefer to hand it over to an expert, as there are some affordable options around. Doing the ground work now will save you money.

Always proofread EVERYTHING you write to save embarrassment or misunderstanding later.

To do:

Design your website on paper. How is it going to look, what is it going to do, what are you going to say and how is it all going to link together? Build your website or hand it over to an expert.

Our experiences:

Lucy: "When I first decided to have a website my business was in its infancy. I didn't have money to spend getting it done professionally. I knew little about website design but with the help of friends and site wizards I produced a passable website that has developed through the years. The amount of time I've put into it wouldn't have been cost effective had my business been busier. If I was starting now, I would consider getting it designed professionally as this service is so much more competitively priced."

Julie: "My website has gone through all sorts of changes over the last few years. It's always had the same functionality but the look and professionalism has evolved. It's grown up with the company. It's gone from being a toddler stumbling around to a teenager with an "I can't do any better so this will have to do" attitude. It's now an adult who has confidence, a professional air and won't settle for second best."

BONUS TASK - SENDING TRAFFIC TO YOUR WEBSITE

Constantly send potential customers to your website.
- Post links on Twitter
- Post links on Facebook
- Post links in your newsletter
- Put your website address on all stationery
- Put your website address in your email signature
- Put your website address in all forum profiles and signatures
- Put your website address on all advertising

Notepad

Task 13: Blogs

Do you have a blog that you are posting on regularly? Does it project the personality you've created for your business? Are your posts being commented on and shared?

A blog is a vital part of your website. It is your own online magazine containing regular articles, features, competitions and reviews. As it's your magazine it needs to look like it belongs to your company, reflecting your branding. Over the coming months and years it will become a useful back catalogue of information for customers to browse, making them aware that you are an expert in your field.

Once you have a blog you need to make regular, interesting and informative posts so your visitors will want to read, revisit and share what you're saying. Your posts should contain links to guide readers to other relevant areas of your website so they are only ever one click away from the information they need.

Your blog should include:
- Reviews of products
- Competitions
- New product ideas

- Offers
- Current trends and your take on what's going on in your industry
- News and information

Don't panic – you aren't suddenly going to have to start writing lots of extra new articles for your blog. You can adapt what you write so one idea can be used across social media, newsletters and blog posts. For example, you tweet that the latest nail colours are being released on Wednesday. When they arrive you post a photo on Facebook showing they're here and you can't wait to start offering them to customers. On Thursday your blog post could be a more in-depth introduction to each colour and photographs to show what they all look like. (At this point tweet and post on Facebook a link to your blog.) When you send out your next newsletter it can re-iterate information from your blog with a special offer (tweet and Facebook a link to your newsletter). You've used one piece of news eight times, showing how easy it is keeping your business in people's minds. And if you can create a news story like this from such a small event imagine what else you could start writing about!

Each of your blog posts is on the internet and serves as an advertisement for you. Each word you write could be picked up when somebody uses a search engine so make sure you include words that are key to your business. If a florist writes a blog post showing the flowers she supplied for a wedding she could mention the event, the venue, the flowers she used and where the cake came from that she decorated. In future, when anyone searches that venue, that cake maker, those flowers or her, then her blog post will come up somewhere in those search results.

To do:

Create your blog and make a list of possible ideas and articles you can write. Use past Facebook posts and tweets as inspiration. Aim to publish at least two blog posts a week and promote them on Facebook, Twitter etc. If you know you've got a busy week ahead pre-write your posts and schedule them to be published for you automatically.

Our experiences:

Lucy: "I like to use my blog to show photographs of the latest products that I offer. I then share these blog posts on Twitter and Facebook, which gives me an easy tweet or post to write. This has worked well as a large distributor shared a photograph from my blog post with the thousands of people who like their Facebook page – many people then saw my article, which they wouldn't normally have come across."

Julie: "It's one thing showing customers what our products look like but seeing the reaction they get when they arrive really sells them. For this reason we like to include customer and blogger reviews as blog posts. This shows potential customers exactly what to expect from one of our deliveries. Once a review is live on our blog we always share the link on Facebook and Twitter, giving that post an even wider audience."

BONUS TASK - REMEMBER TARGETS

How are you doing with those targets?
- Are you still taking steps to move towards them?
- Have you identified the next steps that you need to take?
- When you reach a target set your next one

If you feel you need extra support setting up a blog visit
www.thesmallbusinessjigsaw.co.uk

Notepad

Task 14: Maximising Time

How much time do you waste every day? Are you as efficient as you could be?

Why work more hours than you need to? The more efficient you can be the fewer hours you need to work. Being efficient could mean setting up systems to reduce production time, grouping tasks together or organising your space better so you don't waste time looking for things.

Whatever your business there will be jobs that you can prepare in advance. If you are a balloon artist working at children's parties you could group together balloons that you're going to use for the same sculptures so they're quick to grab.

Group tasks together. If you have phone calls to make, sit down and do them all at the same time. If you need to go to the bank, are there any other jobs you can do on your way back?

Be strict with yourself. Make sure you don't waste time online. Social media may be entertaining in your own time but whilst you're logged on for work focus on looking for and talking to the right people about the

right things. Get used to using social media apps like
Hootsuite.com, which allows you to schedule tweets in
advance so you're not tempted to spend 20 minutes
seeing what your friends have been up to.

To do:

Look at what you do, how you do it and how long it
takes. Can you refine any processes? Which tasks can
you group together to save time? Be disciplined in
everything you do, especially when using social media.

Our experiences:

*Lucy: "I used to make regular trips out to different
wholesalers. I decided to use my stock take list to
identify what was running out and use two online
wholesalers instead. This saves me time and money,
as I am no longer spending half a morning driving to
get one thing I need. I use that time to fit in extra
clients."*

*Julie: "We sell an awful lot of balloon flower
bouquets so we make loads of flowers every week.
They're always the same colours so now if we get
any spare time at the beginning of the week we spend
it making extra flowers. This means that we only
need to put them into bouquets when an order comes*

in. It saves us a lot of time. If we end up with unsold flowers we can always use them to promote the company by giving them away to local offices or as a competition prize on Facebook or Twitter."

BONUS TASK: FILL AN EXTRA HOUR

Don't waste time. Make a list of jobs that will take less than an hour and fit them in when the opportunity arises.

- Think of a cancellation or quiet afternoon as an opportunity to complete some of these jobs
- Small jobs could include sorting out your receipts, tidying your stock cupboard, leafleting etc.
- Add to your list anything you can prepare in advance
- Catch up with work emails or social media on your phone when queuing in the post office or waiting to pick up the kids, etc.

Notepad

Task 15: Maximising Profit

What are your most and least profitable lines? Where could you make more profit? What should you discontinue?

You should know, to the penny, what every product you sell or service you offer costs you. It will help you get rid of deadwood...the parts of your business that are making you very little profit or even costing you money.

When you have calculated the cost of everything you do, look at your profit margins and list them from the most to the least profitable. You need to sell more of the things that are making you the most profit and consider dropping the things that there is little point continuing to sell. Remember to consider the time factor in your costings. It might look like you are making a large profit but if it takes five hours to make, pack and post an item, you may have no profit at all.

Before you drop a product or service see if you can make it more profitable by changing suppliers or streamlining how you work. Alternatively, are you charging enough? If you increase the price, you increase your profit – but don't price yourself out of the market.

If none of this is possible, you should seriously consider getting rid of that deadwood.

To do:

Work out the cost of every product or service you offer, including materials and time. Look at your profit margins – can you increase these by getting a better deal on materials, streamlining your time or charging more? Aim to sell more of the most profitable items and drop those that aren't cost effective.

Our experiences:

> Lucy: "I leave a certain amount of time for each treatment I do. I realised that sometimes I was over estimating the time I should allow because I was new to that treatment and wasn't sure how long it would take. I streamlined how I did things so it ran more smoothly and I found I could fit in an extra appointment each day, so my business benefited."

> Julie: "This task was invaluable. It made me re-cost every sculpture and look at exactly how much we made each time we sold one via our site or a trade

customer. Some designs were dropped from our range instantly, whilst it became clear that we were undercharging for others. Our profitability increased overnight."

BONUS TASK: SCHEDULING TIME

A well-organised schedule will make you more efficient, more realistic about what you can achieve each day and make your customers happier.

- Respect other people's time – always be on time for appointments
- Appointments can over run so build a contingency into your schedule
- Be realistic about how long a task takes
- Be practical about how much work you can take on in one day
- Schedule in breaks throughout the day

Notepad

Task 16: Maximising Sales

How can you increase the value of each sale? Are there any products or services that naturally add on to existing sales? Can you increase the number of returning customers?

Getting an additional sale or bigger sale from an existing customer is much easier and cheaper than finding a new one. When a customer purchases an item or service, is there something else you could suggest they add to their 'shopping cart'? Enhance their experience by making them aware of additional complementary products. For example, if you're a photographer who specialises in canvas prints do your customers know you also print mugs, key rings and other products with the same design?

Look at creating packages. If you offer cooking lessons, at your next Italian Cooking Experience how about bundling up essential ingredients and utensils for your students to purchase so they can start cooking the same authentic Italian dishes as soon as they get home.

You could create a bundle and offer a discount if a customer purchases a number of services at the same time.

Is there anything obvious you can buy in to optimise sales? A manicurist could retail hand cream after a manicure or offer an add-on treatment such as nail art.

If you're considering adding a new product do your homework; don't act on impulse. Upselling might feel strange at first but it will quickly become second nature as you start to see the positives response you get.

Repeat customers are an important way to maximise income. Good customer service and keeping in contact is the key. Letting existing customers know about new products, special offers and sales will give them an excuse to keep coming back. This can be done via social media, emails and newsletters. If you're in a service industry it is as simple as asking them when they would like their next appointment before they leave.

To do:

Look at what you offer and which products naturally link together to provide add-ons or packages. Promote these using Twitter, Facebook, a website page etc. Stay in touch with your customers so it is easier for them to buy again. Encourage clients to rebook where appropriate.

Our experiences:

> *Lucy: "I discovered that clients who were having CND shellac manicures were buying similar coloured polish elsewhere to paint their toenails. I invested in CND Vinylux, which can be retailed, so clients could buy polish that was an exact match directly from me. This has proved very popular."*

> *Julie: "Adding a personal message is part and parcel of the service that we offer. It's an important part of every delivery. Messages are written on a note card and held by our Balloon Baboon mascot.*

> *We wanted to make these messages even more special so we looked around for ideas. We settled on a Message in a Bottle. We now offer customers the option, for a fee, to have their message written on a tiny scroll and popped in a mini corked bottle containing confetti hearts, also held by a Balloon Baboon mascot. These have proved incredibly popular, not only increasing the value of many orders but also making the delivery even cuter."*

BONUS TASK - CUSTOMER SERVICES

Always over-deliver:
- Go the extra mile
- Consider adding an extra little freebie
- Only promise what you know you can deliver
- Remind the customer if you have an offer on that will save them money

Notepad

Task 17: Newsletter

Have you got a newsletter that you send out regularly? Do your subscribers open, read and act on them?

This task isn't about how to create a newsletter – there are plenty of websites like Mailchimp.com that will guide you through that process. This is about how to make the most of this valuable tool.

A great newsletter can help build a stronger relationship with your customers. As with all marketing, your newsletter must reflect the image and personality of your business – that's right, the colour, logo and design that we keep harping back to as they're so important!

Your newsletter should be useful and interesting so people want to open it. It needs to be concise and to the point – too wordy and they'll press delete and may unsubscribe from your list.

Choose your subjects wisely. They could be snippets of information, articles, sneak previews and special offers. Whatever you pick, remember the golden rule: useful, interesting and concise.

Newsletters should be regular so your subscribers don't forget you. If you know you're going to have a busy month plan ahead and write them in advance.

Planning is vital. To reduce your workload you could link some of your stories to upcoming events. If you're a chocolatier your January newsletter could have Valentine stories and offers, February's issue could reflect Mother's Day etc. Every business will have their own milestones but you can also be inventive. What about obscure National Days – if you help people de-clutter their home the 10th of May is Clean Up Your Room Day. 13th August is Blame Someone Else Day – perfect for a solicitor. What national days or events could you link to in your newsletter?

It's no good writing the perfect newsletter if you have no one to send it to. Make sure you have a sign-up form on your website and your 'contact' form allows people to opt in to receive it. Let people know about your newsletter via Facebook, Twitter and other social media networks. Ask your customers if they want to receive it. Even if you already have their email address you need their permission to send it to them.

Newsletters need to get customers to take action by contacting you, making a purchase or finding out more. Get your newsletter right and people will want to click through to your offers, share them and recommend them to their friends.

To do:

Design the perfect newsletter for your company. Plan ahead, deciding what information you want to include in the next and future issues. Put the dates you're going to send them out in your diary. Encourage new subscribers to sign up to your newsletter through your website, via social media etc.

Our experiences:

Lucy: "I didn't have a newsletter so this task made me panic! I signed up to Mailchimp and their easy-to-follow tutorial soon had me producing professional-looking newsletters. I use it to promote new product releases and treatments and include a monthly special offer that always proves to be popular."

Julie: "As predominately a gift company it makes sense for us to link the content of our newsletters to events throughout the year. Valentine's and Mother's Day have always been incredibly busy but we also see an increase in sales when we suggest gifts for other less obvious events. We now sell a lot of miniature Graduates in June and July and Halloween masks made out of balloons in October. These sales have only come about because we have suggested they would make great novelty buys at those times of the year."

Notepad

Task 18: Rewarding Customers

Do your customers know that you value them? Do you reward their loyalty?

You should always pursue new customers but it is more cost effective to retain the ones you have. They've chosen to use you, which is a huge compliment, and you need to say thank you with great customer service and reliability.

There are numerous ways to thank customers for their loyalty: refer a friend schemes, money off vouchers, thank you gifts, free postage etc. – none of these cost a fortune. Use your imagination and you will encourage a loyal customer base.

Look at setting up a loyalty scheme, but weigh up the cost to your business. If you're going to give £10 back with every completed loyalty card how much do your customers need to spend to make it worth your while?

There is nothing more annoying to a loyal customer if they feel new customers are being treated better than they are. Reward them both.

Newsletters are the perfect way to let existing customers find out about new services and products before anyone else. Treat them to sneak previews so they feel valued.

To do:

Set up a loyalty scheme that suits your business and promote it. Make a list of different ways you are going to thank your customers and make them feel appreciated. Take steps to implement your list.

Our experiences:

Lucy: "Many of my new customers are referred to me by existing clients so I wanted to say thank you. I have seen schemes where only the new client is rewarded but I wanted to thank the person who was kind enough to recommend me. I devised a 'refer a friend' card. When produced, both the new and old client receive a £5 discount. This has been really popular and encouraged my clients to talk about me."

Julie: "A lot of our business comes from repeat customers. Not only have we set up a very popular loyalty scheme but also a Fan Club, to say thank you. To join the Fan Club customers pay £5 and get 10% off every order for a year. With so many people coming back time and time again it's nice to be able to give them another way to save money."

Notepad

Task 19: Low Cost Advertising

What is your advertising strategy? How much is it costing you?

You can spend hundreds of pounds on advertising if you have a large budget but is it the best way when you could use effective low cost advertising instead?

The cheapest way to increase your customer base is through word of mouth so it's important to encourage loyal customers to recommend you. Your impeccable customer service should mean that customers will instinctively refer their friends to you. You can encourage this by offering the incentives you devised in *Reward Your Customers' Loyalty* (Chapter 18).

Slightly more expensive is leaflet distribution. To get the most from your leaflets they should be well designed, with your company branding and the right copy. They should make people want to contact you. Traditionally, leaflets can result in a low response rate but this increases if they are well designed and target the right audience. If you have spare time you have nothing to lose.

Don't just deliver leaflets door to door – find places where you can leave a pile. Are there any large companies near you, or related industries? If you're a wedding photographer you could swap leaflets with a florist.

Leaflets can also be sent out in any parcels, put in welcome packs for new clients and handed to existing customers. If you find that leafleting works for you but you start to run out of time pay a distribution company. However you do it, make sure those leaflets go out as they're no good if they're sitting in a drawer.

You should now have a highly effective online business presence. You are communicating with your customers, followers and fans via social media pages – but you can make those pages work even harder. Look for influential bloggers to review your products and journalists who are looking for someone just like you for an article they are writing.

Increase your online presence with other tools such as Pinterest, Instagram, LinkedIn or free online directories. It could be useful to exchange reciprocal links with related industries.

Find busy forums that are associated with your business or target audience. Become an active member and offer support and advice whenever possible. In time you will become perceived as an expert and people will gravitate towards you and your website.

Remember, for maximum results you should have a combination of advertising strategies in place rather than concentrating on one.

To do:

Make a list of relevant forums, social media sites and directories. Create a profile even if you use some more than others. If you don't already have leaflets get one designed and start distributing them. Promote your 'refer a friend' / recommendation scheme.

Our experiences:

Lucy: "When I started my business I delivered leaflets door to door despite being told they wouldn't be effective. I decided as I had the time I may as well put my headphones on, walk the dog and get out and do something proactive. I knew my potential clients would be local so I targeted a three mile radius from my clinic. I received a 4% response rate and of those people who booked in for treatments, many are still clients 20 years later."

Julie: "One of the #hashtags on Twitter that we keep an eye on is #journorequest. It's where journalists post requests for products, information or experts they need for articles they are working on. Every now and then we stumble on a tweet that we can respond to with an offer of help. In some cases it has led to some incredible free press coverage for our products."

Notepad

Task 20: Do You Know Who I Am?

Do people know what you do? Are you telling them when you get the opportunity?

You could have the most amazing business in the world but if you don't tell people about it then it won't succeed. Whether it's an unjustified lack of confidence, a difficulty in explaining the complexities of your business or something completely different you have to get over it!

How many times has someone asked for your contact number and you stand there patting your pockets and searching your bag? You always need to have your business cards with you.

Here's a little trick...have printed some business cards that are blank on the back, or small message cards with your company name, tagline and website. Use these cards to write down phone numbers, notes, bus times, restaurant recommendations, anything. You have given someone the information they needed but they also have your business details. You never know when they might use them.

And now for 'networking'. For most people this conjures up a room full of strangers that you know you should go and talk to. Go to those events but remember, networking is bigger than that. Every time you meet someone, you can potentially talk about what you do, should the opportunity arise. However, there is a fine line between giving them basic information and delivering a pushy sales pitch.

You're already networking online by using Facebook and Twitter. On Twitter, related businesses come together for an hour at a set time each week to talk about what they do and the latest news in their field. Each tweet contains a common hashtag e.g. #reflexologyhour or #handmadehour. There are also hashtags concentrating on locality.

The nearest equivalent on Facebook are 'like ladders', where similar businesses share their pages for others to view and 'like'. Etiquette suggests you then like their page in return. There are also Facebook pages based on locality or services that are worth getting involved with.

Both are great ways of making new contacts.

Forums are another online networking opportunity where you can take advantage of some *Low Cost Advertising* (Chapter 19).

To do:

Create business cards that have room for you to scribble messages on – and use them. Find opportunities to tell people what you do and give them your contact details. Use social media to find #hashtags, ladders etc. to increase your profile online. Research forums, join in the discussions and start your own threads.

Our experiences:

> *Lucy: "When writing this task I realised there were many #hashtags on Twitter for other areas near me but not for my local town. I decided to try and encourage #Handforth. Within minutes several local businesses had responded and we started to support each other by retweeting and commenting on each other's tweets. I also received two bookings almost immediately and will definitely continue to promote #Handforth."*

> *Julie: "The simple message cards that we designed to be used with our deliveries are absolutely perfect to carry around and use whenever I want to give someone a piece of information that I would usually write on a scrap of paper. I've used them to write down a book title for someone, the name of a*

restaurant and all sorts of other things. Each of the people I've given those cards to goes away with our website address and a little bit of information about what we do."

BONUS TASK - BUSINESS CARDS

From now on you will always have a business card to hand out. Always keep cards:
- In every pocket
- In every bag
- In every purse or wallet
- In your car
- Everywhere!

Notepad

Task 21: Dealing With The Public

Do you give a good impression to your customers? What are you portraying in person and online? How do you deal with problems and complaints?

There are two sides to customer services: direct contact with customers, and online contact. In person, it is always important to greet your customers with a smile, treat them as you'd want to be treated and answer the phone professionally.

Online you could have an audience of thousands and they are all potential customers who can see how you deal with things. Problems that crop up may no longer be dealt with privately. Think about how you respond, review it and only then press send.

Anyone can write anything about you online – it may be on a review site or their own blog – and some of it might not seem fair. However, you still need to deal with this professionally. If you're replying to a comment that has touched a nerve it is worth walking away and composing your reply after you've had time to reflect. You are always on show so everything you write must be impeccable.

Without the correct security settings anyone can see your personal social media accounts too. As great as that drunken night out was, think twice before uploading those photographs. Is this the image you want to portray? What you do reflects on your company.

Your business may be online 24/7 but whilst some comments may need an immediate response not all do. Tweet and post messages to suit you; manage your time, rather than letting social media manage you.

To do:

Remind yourself what image you want your business to portray and make sure you consistently do this in a professional and friendly way. This includes speaking in person, online, over the phone or on paper.

Our experiences:

> Lucy: *"On Twitter I noticed that a client had put a message saying her polish hadn't lasted on her toes and she was disappointed because she was going on holiday. I quickly responded and asked what had happened and she said she had stubbed her toe and the polish had chipped. I told her to pop in later that day and we could fix it. She was very happy and several of her followers commented on my good*

service. Had I ignored her or told her it was her own fault and nothing to do with me I wouldn't have received that good feedback – and all it cost me was ten minutes of my time."

Julie: "Royal Mail can occasionally let us down and not deliver one of our sculptures on the requested delivery date. Despite acknowledging this possibility on our site, it can understandably be upsetting to a customer if it happens. On one occasion a customer decided to express her upset via a tweet rather than calling or emailing us directly. We expressed our apologies via Twitter and asked her to pass on her details so that we could look into things for her. The rest of the conversation took place via email. Once everything was resolved our customer kindly sent out another tweet praising our prompt customer service and this was re-tweeted via a few of her followers. She has since become a valued repeat customer."

Notepad

Well done...

You've now completed *The Small Business Jigsaw* and have effective strategies in place to help you run your business more effectively. A good way to measure your success so far is to compare where you are now with the Wish List that you created in task one, *First Things First* (Chapter One).

This is just the beginning of your business journey. It would be wonderful – though it's unlikely – if you've ticked off every wish on that initial list. That list might even have changed.

To stay on track and continue working towards your goals you need to keep re-visiting and adjusting tasks and the way they fit into your business. Things will and do change – and that's okay – but you need to move with those changes.

You should be giving yourself a pat on the back. You've had the motivation and courage to set up your business. You've put in a lot of hard work and now it's time to start enjoying the benefits.

You've done really well. Be proud.

Come and share your success stories at
thesmallbusinessjigsaw.co.uk

Fancy a few more bonus tasks?

BONUS TASK: LOVE YOUR WORKSPACE

Whatever your workspace consists of, it is yours. You need to feel comfortable, happy and focused when you are in it.

- Organise your workspace so you know where everything is
- Make it a space you enjoy being in
- Ensure you can walk away at the end of your working day – even if this means packing everything into boxes in a cupboard

BONUS TASK: PLANNING FREE TIME

At your busiest times of the year you may not be able to take time off but...

- If there's something you don't want to miss put it in your diary and work round it if you possibly can
- Even if you only manage a few hours a week get into the habit of taking some time off
- Could you employ someone else so the business doesn't stop when you do?
- Take control of your diary – don't let it control you

BONUS TASK: CELEBRATION

By keeping reminders of the things that make you smile you'll always have a treasure trove of memories to reignite your enthusiasm and remind yourself why you run your own business.

- Choose a box that you like the look of, or a plain one you want to personalise
- Collect testimonials, articles you've written, reviews, thank you cards and anything else that reminds you of your achievements
- As good things happen, continue to add them to your box
- When you need a boost look through the box at all the wonderful things you've achieved

Notepad

About the author ... Lucy Dempster

After finishing university Lucy worked in television for a number of years but she soon realised she didn't want to work long hours for somebody else. She was encouraged to try reflexology and, intrigued by the results and wanting a better understanding of the therapy, she went on to study with the late Clive O'Hara.

Over the years she has increased the treatments she offers to include aromatherapy, hot stone massage and CND Shellac nail treatments. She has a particular interest in complementary therapies and cancer care, and she also volunteers at East Cheshire Hospice.

Lucy continues to run a successful business from a clinic at her home and looks forward to future writing projects.

www.holisticandbeautytreatments.co.uk
www.twitter.com/onlyholistic
www.facebook.com/HolisticandBeautybylucydempster

About the author ... Julie Hayward

Julie started her first business in 1997 after seeing a market for second-hand wedding dresses. After finding two independent manufacturers, she then began importing her own range of bridal wear.

In 2010 it was time for a new challenge. Having been shown how to make a basic balloon flower she saw the potential for a new type of balloon delivery company. Balloon Baboon was born. Inspired by some of the world's best balloon twisters, a wide range of sculptures now feature on the company website. In the future Julie plans to offer helium balloon deliveries, balloon training and event decor with a difference.

www.balloonbaboon.co.uk
www.twitter.com/balloonbaboon
www.facebook.com/balloonbaboon